AN EXTRAORDINARY COLLECTION OF CURIOUS CREATURES

BRANDONHAYESART.COM

ISBN 13: 978-1977871305
WWW.BRANDONHAYESART.COM

For my wife and best friend Lara, without you, this would never have been made. Thank you for being you.
To my kids Noel and Jack, for keeping life crazy.

Once the crime was committed, there was no turning back.
My face is in the papes, they are on my track.
Hiding and so close to being caught.
How I fear all this will be for naught.
Money for the shop and flowers for amends.
The time has finally come, now it all must end.
A gavel and a roar almost make me regret.
Oh what I do for my love, my dear Lennette.

MORTIMERS
MORSELS
DOTTYS
COLORED
DOTS
Candy
Straws
Super
Squares
Super
Scrumptious
SLICES
Penny Penguins
Sweet Shoppe
ASSORTED
BAG OF BONES
BAG OF BONES
BAG OF BONES
BAG OF BONES
BAG OF BONES
RISKY
GOLD BAR
GUMMY
BEARS

BANK
HARRISON POLICE

Clucky

HERALD
SUSPECT IN BANK ROBBERY
INK
BEE KEEPING
THE SIGNS

TATTOOS
FLO
FLOR
MOM

Flora's Florals
ORDER ROSCOE SOWES

APOTHECARY
POL

HARRISON HER
BANK ROBBER NABBED
BAKE
HOTEL
HERALD
BAKERY OPENING

HARRISON COUNTY ZOO
042487
ROSCOE "SMOKING GUN" JON

www.ingramcontent.com/pod-product-compliance
Lightning Source LLC
Chambersburg PA
CBHW080728260726
48660CB00010B/3749